KOBLENZ: CITY AND HISTORY

The Roman camp "Castellum apud Confluentes" was originally established between 10 and 8 BC, under the reign of Augustus. In the course of time the name was abbreviated to Confluentia, and finally Koblenz. The city was a royal court in the 5th century, and in 1018 it became the property of the Archbishops of Trier. Koblenz's heyday was between the 12th and 14th centuries. It fell to the French at the end of the 18th century and then to the Prussians in 1815. Much of the city was razed and destroyed during World War II. In 1992 Koblenz celebrated its 2,000th anniversary with many colourful events and attractions. In 1993, after much heated debate and extensive planning, a faithful copy of the huge equestrian statue of Kaiser Wilhelm I destroyed in the War was cast in bronze and installed on the old base at the Deutsches Eck ("German Corner"). Today, Koblenz is located in the state of Rhineland-Palatinate (Rheinland-Pfalz) and is one of the

Görresplatz (square) with "Historiensäule" ▽

most beautifully situated cities in Europe. It has grown to take up the entire valley plain between the Rhine and the Moselle. Incorporation of other communities has further extended the city to the north and west of the Moselle and east of the Rhine. The city centre lies on a tongue of land between the Rhine and the Moselle, with the rest of the city, the industrial area and the Rhine port directly adjacent. Koblenz is an important intersection of many transport routes and the seat of a number of federal and state authorities. It is also a major economic centre; among other things, Koblenz is one of the leading wine trading cities on the Rhine. The German Army has its biggest national base here, with facilities including the Federal Defence Technology Office and the Army Purchasing Agency. Koblenz has always been a city of the arts, and it has plenty to offer for those interested in culture and history. The sights include many churches and historical monuments from wide arange of periods, a variety

▽ Koblenz, Deutsches Eck ("German Corner", at the point where the Moselle flows into the Rhine)

of museums, theatres and concert halls with a rich programme of events. There are also many opportunities for leisure activities and sports in and around Koblenz, including hiking trails, river cruises and excursions into the beautiful surrounding countryside. The magnificent Rhine Promenades and the many picturesque corners of the city just waiting to be discovered round off the list of attractions. The Old Town ist particularly attractive. Its beautiful old houses have now been lovingly restored, and the excellent shops are an added attraction, making a stroll through the charming old streets really worthwhile. Koblenz has a wealth of restaurants and wine bars where you can enjoy the excellent Rhine and Moselle wines. The most popular varieties are the whites made from the famous Riesling, Silvaner and Müller-Thurgau grapes. This fascinating city on the Rhine and Moselle is well worth a visit, as is confirmed by the countless tourists who come here every year.

CHRONOLOGY OF THE HISTORY OF KOBLENZ

FROM 1800 BC
Many settlements in the area around Koblenz.

BETWEEN 10 AND 8 BC
Establishment of the Roman camp "Confluentes" at the confluence of the Rhine and the Moselle. The city of Koblenz grew up around this camp.

1ST CENTURY AD
Koblenz grows, but is also destroyed several times. Establishment of further camps in the vicinity.

3RD CENTURY
Destruction of the fort of Niederberg by the Franks in 259.

4TH CENTURY
To protect themselves against the attacks of the Franks the Romans build a high ring wall around Koblenz, with 19 round towers.

5TH CENTURY
At the beginning of the C5 the Franks overcome the Romans and destroy the city. The Franks then rebuild Koblenz at the end of the C5 and establish their royal court here.

CIRCA 1000
The knight Ehrembert builds the first castle known by the name of Ehrenbreitstein.

1018
Kaiser Heinrich II gives the royal court of Koblenz to Archbishop Poppo of Trier as a present, also granting him the right to mint coins and levy tolls.

13TH CENTURY
The Knights of the Teutonic Order (Deutscher Orden) become established in Koblenz in 1216. The Knights build an entire complex for the Order at the confluence of the Rhine and the Moselle, after which the spit of land is known as the "Deutsches Eck" ("German Corner").

1250–1300
Construction of the city walls and fortifications (some remains of which survive today).

1343
Archbishop Balduin, who reigned in Koblenz from 1307 to 1354, commences construction of the Moselle bridge.

16TH CENTURY
The Jesuits settle in Koblenz and establish the Jesuit grammar school in 1582.

17TH CENTURY
During the Thirty Years' War (1618–1648) Koblenz is taken by the French and then by the Swedes. Finally, the city is retaken by the Kaiser's army, but suffers severe devastation in the process.

1688
Following reconstruction, Koblenz is once again partially destroyed, this time by the troops of Louis XIV.

FROM 1690
Royal seat of the Prince-Electors (Kurfürsten) of Trier.

1780–1786
Koblenz Castle is built at the behest of Prince-Elector (Kurfürst) Clemens Wenzeslaus of Saxony, who reigned from 1768 to 1794.

1794
The city is taken by the French revolutionary troops and Wenzeslaus flees, bringing the Trier Electorate to an end.

1798
Koblenz becomes the Prefecture of the French "Rhin et Moselle" department.

1814/1815
Koblenz becomes Prussian, following Napoleon's defeat and the redivision of Europe at the Congress of Vienna.

1822–1832
Construction of the Prussian city fortifications.

1890
Surrender of the city fortifications.

1897
Inauguration of the Kaiser Wilhelm I monument at the Deutsches Eck.

1944
Severe devastation of the city at the climax of World War II.

1945
Destruction of the equestrian statue of Kaiser Wilhelm I.

1947–1950
Koblenz becomes the capital of the state of Rhineland-Palatinate, but then has to rescind this position to Mainz.

JULY 8, 1948
The foundation of the Federal Republic of Germany is resolved on Rittersturz hill in Koblenz.

1957
The French Army begins its withdrawal, bringing its twelve-year occupation of the city to an end.

1974
Opening of the new Moselle bridge (Europabrücke) following enlargement and renovation.

1983
Building excavation reveals the remains of C3 and C4 AD Roman fortifications and baths.

1992
Celebrations marking the city's 2,000th anniversary.

SEPTEMBER 2, 1993
Europe's biggest floating crane lifts the faithful copy of the original equestrian statue of Kaiser Wilhelm I into position on the pedestal at the Deutsches Eck.

SEPTEMBER 25, 1993
Official inauguration of the equestrian statue of Kaiser Wilhelm I at the Deutsches Eck.

DEUTSCHES ECK

The "Deutsches Eck" ("German Corner") lies on a spit of land at the point where the Moselle flows into the Rhine. The name originates from the Knights of the Teutonic Order (Deutscher Orden), who settled and established their first centre here in 1216. Following banking-up of the promontory at the end of the 19th century, the government of the Rhine Province (Rheinprovinz) built a monument to Kaiser Wilhelm I here, commemorating the victory of 1871. The construction took from 1883 to 1897. The project was proposed by the city councillors Julius Wegeler and Franz Adams, a few weeks after the Kaiser's death. A call for donations brought in 80,000 marks from the public. It was Kaiser Wilhelm II who decided the final location of the monument; the parliament of the province had originally chosen the Drachenfels rock overlooking Königswinter. A total of six million gold marks were spent on the project. Overall, the monument was 37 metres high, making it

Equestrian statue of Kaiser Wilhelm I ▽

even taller than the Niederwald monument near Rüdesheim. The 14-metre equestrian statue of the Kaiser was cast from 35,000 kg of copper ingots and stood on a columned hall 10 metres high. The Kaiser's gaze faced downriver, the horse's tail towards the arch-enemy, France. After standing here for 48 years, the monument was destroyed during World War II, on March 16, 1945. Horse and rider tipped over to the right to hang head down from the base of the monument. Initially, the Koblenzers did nothing to save their fallen Kaiser, as they had other problems. Then the statue simply disappeared, creating a great sensation. To this day, no one knows who was behind the "kidnapping", or why and how they did it. The monument was initially redesigned without the statue and its accompanying group of figures by mounting the coats of arms of Germany's federal states along the semicircular south wall. The Kaiser's "W" with his sword and hand in the gesture of oath are still visible above the coats of arms.

▽ *Deutsches Eck/Equestrian statue of Kaiser Wilhelm I – overall height of the monument: 37 m*

In 1953, Germany's President Theodor Heuss declared the monument to be a "Memorial to German Unity". The first calls to replace the statue of Kaiser Wilhelm I came a number of years later, but the state government in Mainz was opposed to the idea. Citizens' groups supporting and opposing a new statue were formed. In 1987, a Koblenz publisher made an impressive offer to the state Rhinland-Palatinate, which had inherited the Deutsches Eck: He said he would finance a copy of the original statue and give it to the city of Koblenz as a present. The state government rejected this offer as well, but the Koblenz city administration was delighted at the idea. After much toing and froing, the state government donated the Deutsches Eck to the city of Koblenz. And on September 2, 1993, Europe's biggest floating crane lifted the faithful 61.5-ton bronze copy of the equestrian statue of Kaiser Wilhelm I onto its restored pedestal.

Height of the equestrian statue: 14 m; weight: 61.5 t (copper-bronze alloy); height of the Genius figure: 9 m; wings: 5 m ▽

◁▽ *Deutsches Eck ("German Corner")*   *Ehrenbreitstein Fortress and the equestrian statue of Kaiser Wilhelm I (Deutsches Eck)* △

St Castor's Church

(St. Kastor-Kirche) The eastside of Kastor Platz (square) is dominated by the parish church of St Castor (a former Collegiate church), artistically Koblenz's most important sacred building. The remains of the preceding structure, a Carolingian church consecrated in 836, have only been preserved in parts of the foundations. In the 12th century the church was significantly enlarged, with the addition of the two spires, choir and a miniature gallery, flanked by two small spires, all in the Romanesque style. The columned basilica with its three naves was reconsecrated at the beginning of the 13th century. Worth seeing inside the building: the tombs of the Prince-Electors Kuno von Falkenstein and Werner von Königstein, lying beneath Gothic wall canopies, and the impressive bronze crucifix (cast in 1685) above the high altar. The early Baroque stone pulpit (1625) is also interesting. The Kastor Fountain in the square in front of the church was built in 1794.

◁▽ *St Castor's Church*

DEUTSCHHERRENHAUS (LUDWIG MUSEUM)

The Knights of the Teutonic Order (Deutscher Orden) built their first centre here in 1216, with the support of Archbishop Dietrich II of Trier. As of 1792, the Deutschherrenhaus served as a barracks and magazine, and in 1895 the State Archive was installed here. Much of the complex was destroyed in World War II, but parts were restored in 1953. Since 1992 it has been the home of the Ludwig Museum, devoted primarily to post-war French art.

▽ *Deutschherrenhaus (Ludwig Museum)*

FOUR TOWERS – LÖHRSTRASSE

The "Four Towers" are actually four houses with lovely stone oriels, flanking the crossroads of the Marktstrasse and Löhrstrasse. Following the destruction of the city by the French in 1688, a uniform design was used for the restoration of the old buildings and the addition of new ones. The St Peter House (1691) stands on the south side, with the Green Tree House (Haus zum Grünen Baum, 1692, rebuilt in 1950) to its left. Haus Raffauf (1608) and the red Haus Eierstock stand on the north side of the crossroads.

Four Towers (Vier Türme) – Löhrstrasse ▷

△▽ *The Old Mint (Alte Münze) – Münzplatz (square)*

THE OLD MINT/MÜNZPLATZ

(Alte Münze) The old Mint Master's house, built by J. Seiz in 1763, still stands on the Münzplatz (square). It used to be the home of the Master of the Electoral Mint. All the other buildings were torn down by the French at the end of the 18th century. Today, the Old Mint is a social centre for senior citizens. Also interesting: Metternicher Hof, the former city court of the Imperial Barons (Reichsfreiherren) of Metternich, a title borne by three clerical Prince-Electors in the 16th and 17th centuries. The shell coat of arms from this period still hangs over the portals. The house was also the birthplace of Clemens Wenceslaus Lothar Prince of Metternich (b. 1773), who was Chancellor of Austria for decades in the first half of the 19th century. Most of the Münzplatz (square) is a pedestrian precinct, and it is the venue of a weekly market. There are number of popular and very pleasant pavement cafés on the square.

"Dä Schoster Hennerich Rech" Monument ▽

PLAN

This square in the Old Town used to be a tournament ground, a place of execution and a meat market. In the 19th century the Town Hall stood here. The historical facades of many of the buildings here are a reminder of old Koblenz, including the former city fire station, the Drouvensche Haus on the east side, the Green Tree House (Haus zum Grünen Baum) and the red Haus Eierstock. Today, people come here to go shopping or to relax with their friends in the restaurants and cafés.

▽ *Plan (square)*

CHURCH OF OUR LADY

(Liebfrauenkirche) The Church of Our Lady in the Old Town has been the principal parish church of the city since the Middle Ages. It dates from a variety of periods. The Romanesque galleried basilica rests on Roman, Carolingian and Frankish foundations and was built in the 12th and 13th centuries. The late-Gothic choir was built in 1404–1431. The Baroque belfries are from the late 17th century. The church was destroyed in World War II but then rebuilt in the original style.

Church of Our Lady (Liebfrauenkirche) ▷

△ Moselle panorama

Old Castle (Alte Burg, 13th century) ▽

OLD CASTLE

(Alte Burg) This imposing siege castle was built in 1276–1289 by Archbishop Heinrich of Trier, but it was not finally completed until the beginning of the 14th century. The building has two towers facing the Moselle and a third for the richly-ornamented spiral staircase built in 1557. In the 15th and 16th centuries the castle was modernised and Renaissance and Baroque style extensions were added. Today the Old Castle houses the City Archive and the City Library.

BALDUIN BRIDGE

(Balduinbrücke) The original bridge was built in the 14th century by Prince-Elector Balduin and had 14 spans (now 11). A stone statue of Balduin still stands in the middle of the bridge. Several spans had to be taken down and replaced with a concrete structure in 1964 when the course of the Moselle was adjusted. The most recent renovation was in 1975. This was not the first bridge over the Moselle here – in 1864 the remains of a Roman pile bridge were discovered 50 metres downriver.

The statue of Prince-Elector Balduin on the Balduin Bridge ▽

ST FLORIN'S CHURCH

(Florinskirche) Built in the 10th and 11th centuries and formerly a Collegiate church, St Florin's is now a Protestant parish church. The Gothic choir was added to the three-naved Romanesque basilica in 1350; the pointed belfries in 1899. The extensive fire damage suffered in World War II has now been repaired; the white and yellow facade dates from 1970. The Middle Rhenish glass paintings and Gothic wall paintings in this plain church are well worth seeing.

OLD MERCHANTS' HALL (MITTELRHEIN-MUSEUM)

(Altes Kaufhaus) The original structure built in 1419–1425 was the city's old merchants' hall. It burned down in 1689 and was rebuilt in 1724. The clock tower harmonises well with the Baroque facade. The Old Merchants' Hall and the Bürresheimer Hof have been the home of the Mittelrhein-Museum since 1965. Exhibits include a city history collection, Baroque sculptures and paintings and works by Dutch and Middle Rhenish painters.

▽ *The "German Kaiser" (Deutscher Kaiser)*

Peter Altmeier Monument ▽

◁ *St Florin's Church (Florinskirche)*

Old Merchants' Hall (Altes Kaufhaus, Mittelrhein-Museum) ▽

DEUTSCHER KAISER

Crowned with battlements, the five-storey, tower-like "Deutscher Kaiser" ("German Kaiser") house was built at the beginning of the 16th century as a residence for the Koblenz Schöffen (a kind of juror) and the masters of the Archbishop's mint. It is the only building in the Old Town that has survived the wars of all the intervening eras unscathed. The late-Gothic net-vaulted ground floor now houses a pub that serves excellent wine.

JESUITENPLATZ/TOWN HALL

The former Jesuit college on the Jesuitenplatz (square) has been the city's Town Hall (Rathaus) since 1895. It has a lovely Renaissance front and was rebuilt around 1700. Worth seeing: beautiful frescos by the Italian Lucaes and stucco work by C. M. Pozzi in the stairwell. The Jesuit church stands on the east side of the square; the severe damage suffered during the War was repaired in 1958/59. Some of the old burgher houses on the square are also interesting.

▽ *Jesuitenplatz (square)*

SCHÄNGEL FOUNTAIN

(Schängelbrunnen) The fountain stands in the courtyard of the present Town Hall, surrounded by Renaissance and Baroque buildings. It was designed by Carl Burger in 1940 and is dedicated to the local Koblenz poet Josef Cornelius (1849–1943). "Schängel" is derived from the French "Jean" and means a young boy or scamp. The fountain is a monument to these mischievous Koblenz scallywags, and the figure offers onlookers a little "entertainment" every two minutes ...

▽ Schängel Fountain (Schängelbrunnen)

Inventors' Fountain/Noah's Ark Fountain △

CITY THEATRE/OBELISK

(Stadttheater) The City Theatre on Deinhardplatz (square) was built in 1787 by Peter Joseph Krahe in the classical style, as a comedy theatre, opera house and assembly hall. Today, operas, operettas and plays are staged here. The building has an interesting front with seven different axes; the empire-style auditorium is horseshoe-shaped. The 19-metre obelisk and the Clemens fountain on the Deinhardplatz were donated by the last Prince-Elector (Kurfürst), Clemens Wenzeslaus.

SACRED HEART CHURCH

(Herz-Jesu-Kirche) Designed by cathedral architect Ludwig Becker from Mainz, the imposing Catholic Sacred Heart Church was built in 1900–1903 on the Moselring. In terms of area it is the biggest Catholic church in the Koblenz city centre. The neo-Romanesque structure was severely damaged in World War II and restored in 1950–1952. Originally, this was the site of the Löhr Tor (Gate), part of the Prussian fortifications torn down in 1897.

▽ *City Theatre (Stadttheater)/Obelisk*   *Sacred Heart Church (Herz-Jesu-Kirche)* ▷

△ The Electoral Palace (Kurfürstliches Schloss)　　　　　　　　　　　　　　　　　　Moselle panorama ▽

ELECTORAL PALACE

(Kurfürstliches Schloss) This big classical-style palace was built in 1777–1786 for the last Prince-Electors (Kurfürsten) of Trier and Archbishop Clemens Wenzeslaus. It was the last German royal residence built in the Middle Rhine region before the French Revolution. From 1849 to 1857 the palace was the seat of the Prussian military governor. In World War II the structure was burned to the ground, but it was rebuilt in 1951. Today it houses the offices of several public authorities.

GÖRRES MONUMENT

(Görresdenkmal) Josef Görres, born here in 1776, was one of Koblenz's greatest sons. The monument dedicated to him in 1928 stands on the Rhine Promenades. Görres was a teacher at the Koblenz grammar school, a journalist and editor of the "Rheinischer Merkur" newspaper. He died in Munich in 1848 while working as professor of history at the university there. An idealised figure entitled "Knowledge" with a book and an eagle stands on a porphyry pedestal with a medallion of Josef Görres.

Görres Monument (Görresdenkmal) ▽

△ Rhein-Mosel-Halle

Rhine Crane (Rheinkran) ▽

RHEIN-MOSEL-HALLE

Located on the square by the Pfaffendorfer bridge, Koblenz's Rhein-Mosel-Halle (Civic Hall) was inaugurated on December 29, 1962. The adjoining hotel was built in the Eighties; together, the complex now forms the Rhine-Moselle Congress Centre. The city's first Civic Hall, built in 1901, also stood on this site; it was destroyed during World War II. Interesting: the fountain in the forecourt with nine basins and a water curtain.

RHINE CRANE/RHINE PROMENADES

(Rheinkran/Rheinanlagen) The old Rhine Crane standing at the beginning of the Rhine Promenades is one of the city's best-known landmarks. Built in 1609–1611, it was originally a crane house and then a water level house. The Rhine Promenades were created at the behest of Empress Augusta; they are among Germany's most beautiful parks. P. J. Lenné, director of the Royal Gardens, was the architect. Today, the Promenades are a popular meeting-spot for locals and tourists from all over the world.

Ehrenbreitstein Fortress (Feste Ehrenbreitstein) ▽

◁ *Vineyard Fountain (Weinbergbrunnen)*

Weindorf △▽

△ *Ehrenbreitstein Fortress (Feste Ehrenbreitstein)*

Rhine in Flames (Rhein in Flammen) ▽

DIKASTERIAL BUILDING

(Dikasterialgebäude) The Dikasterial Building with its beautiful Rococo front stands at the foot of Ehrenbreitstein Fortress. It was built in 1739–1749 for Prince-Elector (Kurfürst) Franz Georg von Schönborn and designed by the famous architect Balthasar Neumann and his student Johannes Seiz. The complex has survived in its original form. It formerly housed the Electoral Government Bureau and the State Planning Authority of Rhineland-Palatinate North.

RHINE IN FLAMES

(Rhein in Flammen) The huge and magnificent spectacel "Rhine in Flames" is held on the second weekend in August every year, bathing the mountains, castles and house fronts from Braubach/Spay to Koblenz in the magical glow of Bengalese fire. Countless ships festooned with lights sail majestically up and down the route. The climax is the grand concluding fireworks show at the fortress of Ehrenbreitstein. There are also a number of folk festivals and fairs at various locations along the riverbanks.

Dikasterial Building (Dikasterialgebäude) ▽

EHRENBREITSTEIN FORTRESS

(Feste Ehrenbreitstein) The original castle of Ehrenbreitstein was built on this 118 metres high hilltop opposite the Deutsches Eck in around 1000 AD. In 1020 the castle came into the possession of the Archbishops of Trier, who fortified it and made a series of additions and extensions. In 1801 the French finally managed to destroy Ehrenbreitstein after a long siege. The Prussians then rebuilt the complex on the original foundations in 1816–1832, adding massive fortifications and batteries to make it Germany's strongest fortress. Today, Ehrenbreitstein houses the Koblenz State Museum (Landesmuseum Koblenz) and the Rhine Museum (Rhein-Museum). There is a wonderful view of Koblenz and the Rhine and Moselle valley from the fortress.

STOLZENFELS CASTLE

(Schloss Stolzenfels) Stolzenfels castle stands high above the Rhine, opposite the confluence of the Lahn. It is one of the most outstanding works of German neo-Gothic romanticism. The first castle was built here in the 13th century. It fell into disrepair after destruction by the French in 1689. Napoleon I bequeathed the ruins to the city in 1802, which then gave it as a present to King Friedrich Wilhelm IV of Prussia in 1823. The King had the castle rebuilt in 1836–1842, with plans drawn up by Karl Friedrich Schinkel, who included the few remaining parts of the complex (e.g. the old keep) in this design. The furnishings installed following this reconstruction have survived. Particularly interesting: the castle courtyard (with a beautiful view), the residential chambers, the knight's halls and the castle chapel.

▽ *Stolzenfels Castle (Schloss Stolzenfels)*